Windows 8

Tips & Apps

Robert Smith

Table of Contents

Part 1

Introduction

Tip 1-Window Charms

Tip 2-Quick Launch Tip

3-Tattoos and Start Screen Color Tip

4-Pin-Ups Tip

5-Semantic Zoom Tip

6-Live Tiles Tip

7-Picture Password Tip

8- Lock Screen Picture

Tip 9-Panoramic Views

Tip 10-Group and Arrange Tiles

Tip 11-Name and Arrange Groups

Tip 12-Tile Size

Tip 13-Desktop Peek

Tip 14-Windows Defender

Tip 15-Shutdown

Tip 16-Desktop Sync

Tip 17-News App

Tip 18-Weather App

Tip 19-Watchlist

Tip 20-Switching to a Microsoft Account

Tip 21-Recover It

Tip 22-SkyDrive

Tip 23-Favorites

Tip 24-Multi Monitor Taskbar

Tip 25-Keyboard Shortcuts

Part 2

Introduction

App 1-Youtube Downloader

App 2-Watchlist

App 3-Netflix

App 4-News Bento

App 5-Podcasts

App 6-Tasks by Telerik

App 7-Skype

App 8-Popular Science

App 9-Music Maker Jam

App 10-Work Notes Pro

App 11-Stumble Upon

App 12-Piktr

App 13-Bing My Lock screen

App 14-Movieoholic

App 15-Tune in Radio

App 16-Typo

App 17-Backgrounds Wallpapers HD

App 18-Norton Satellite

App 19-Storm

App 20-FlipToast

App 21-WorldWeb

App 22-How Stuff Works

App 23-MultiMedia 8

App 24-USA Today

App 25-CNN app for Windows

Part 1

Introduction

Starting with MS-DOS in the 80's Microsoft has since made improvement to its

operating system. The latest version is Windows 8. Windows 95 revolutionized

Microsoft Windows because users no longer had to use the DOS command-line because of a new user-friendly design. Windows 8 is also revolutionary because it introduces major changes including a new "Modern User Interface" (Modern UI) and being able to more easily build web-based touch-enabled apps for PC's, laptops and tablets. Windows 8 has been drastically redesigned.

Part 1 provides tips for Windows 8 to help you learn how to use this new version of Windows. Also included are common Windows 8 keyboard shortcuts. This will improve your Windows 8 experience whether you are a beginner or have been using it for a while.

Tip 1-Window Charms

Charms refer to a menu bar of commonly used system commands and it can be activated from the right side of the screen. Charms include a shortcut back to the start screen plus Search, Share, Devices, and Settings.

Touch Swipe inwards towards the right side of the screen.

Keyboard and Mouse Move the mouse pointer to the upper or lower right corners of the screen towards the charms that appear.

Tip 2-Quick Launch

Microsoft removed the traditional Start button. Instead of using the Start button you should now use the Search charm.

Touch

Swipe inwards towards the right side of the screen to activate the Charms menu. Then tap on the Search charm. By tapping Apps, Settings or Files you can filter the search results.

Keyboard and Mouse

Go to the Start screen and simply start typing to activate the Search charm. By clicking Apps, Settings or Files you can filter the search results.

Tip 3-Tattoos and Start Screen Color

Included in Windows 8 are 25 different color schemes and 20 tattoos that add stylish patterns to the top and bottom of the Start Screen. To change these settings select Settings and then select Change PC Settings. Select Personalize and then select Start Screen.

Tip 4-Pin-Ups

You can pin your favorite apps and files to the start screen for easier access.

Touch

Locate the app with the Search charm and swipe-select on the search result to activate the app command bar, then select Pin to Start.

To pin a file location to the Start Screen, locate a file with the Search charm and swipe-select on the search result to activate the app command bar, then select Open file location. Long-press on the file location to activate the context menu, then select Pin to Start.

Keyboard and Mouse

To pin an app to the Start Screen, locate the app with the Search charm and right click on the search result to activate the command bar, then select Pin to Start.

To pin a file location to the start screen, locate a file with the search charm and right-click on the search result to activate the App command bar, then select Open file location. Right-click on the file location to activate the context menu, then select Pin to Start.

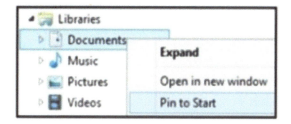

Tip 5-Semantic Zoom

Semantic Zoom provides a high level zoomed out view within many Modern UI

lists, apps and on the Start Screen. This lets you see the overall structure so you

can quickly navigate and browse through content.

Touch Pinch two fingers together on the screen to zoom out, then tap to go to a different

section.

Keyboard and Mouse

Hold the Ctrl key while using the mouse wheel to zoom out, then click on a

different section.

Tip 6-Live Tiles

Live Tiles provide real-time data right on your Start screen, and you don't need to

open any apps. For example, the Weather tile will show you the current conditions,

and Mail will show you the subject of the latest message you've received.

You can customize which apps are live and which aren't by right-clicking on the

tiles. A settings bar on the bottom will open up with an option to turn the Live Tile on or off. Simply select the preferred option, and you're all set. Note, however, that not all apps have a live, real-time data-streaming option.

Tip 7-Picture Password

Using a picture password is a fun way to keep your device secure while not having to remember a complex password. To enable it, press the Windows key + I to get to the settings charm. Tap or Click Change PC settings at the bottom right, and go to the Users tab. Tap or click Sign-in options then tap or click Create a picture password. This will give you the option to choose any picture, and then define three gestures anywhere on the image. Your gestures can be circles, swipes and clicks.

For example, to set a picture password for the image above, you could click on the highest palm tree, draw a circle around the island, and then swipe down from the lens flare in the upper right. Be advised: The direction of each gesture matters. After confirming it a couple times, your picture password will be set.

Tip 8- Lock Screen Picture

When you start Windows 8 the Lock Screen is the first screen you see. You can choose from the six different design Lock Screen images, or you can use one of your own pictures.

Activate the Charms menu, select Settings and then select Change PC Settings. Tap or click to choose a different image or select the Browse button to add your own picture

Tip 9-Panoramic Views

The Travel app allows you to view 360 degree Panoramas of popular tourist locations providing you with an idea of what the place would be like to visit. Activate the Search charm and type in a destination, then tap or click the Search button. Tap or click in the center of the screen to hide the Search charm, then pan or scroll until you see the Panoramas heading. Select a location, tap and hold or click and hold, then drag on the screen to see the full panorama.

Tip 10-Group and Arrange Tiles

You can reorganize the position of the tiles on the Start screen and you can create new groups of tiles.

Touch- To move a tile, press on it and drag your finger up or down to select it, then move the tile to a new location.

To create a new group of tiles drag a tile to an empty area of the Start Screen.

<u>Mouse and Keyboard</u>

To move a tile, click and drag it to a new location.

To create a new group of tiles drag a tile to an empty area of the Start Screen.

Tip 11-Name and Arrange Groups

You can quickly move and label your tile groups using Semantic Zoom. Zoom out to see all your tile groups then drag a group to move it to a new location.

You can label your groups with names. Swipe-select or right-click on a group to activate the App bar, then select Name group, type a description and tap or click Name.

Tip 12-Tile Size

You can change the size of tiles to make your favorite tiles more visible. Swipe select or right click on a tile to activate the App bar and then tap or click on Smaller or Larger to resize the tile.

Tip 13-Desktop Peek

This lets you see your Desktop without closing or minimizing all your open windows.

Touch

Tap & hold your finger in the bottom right corner of the Desktop. When a menu appears, tap the Peek at desktop option, then tap and hold to see a preview of the Desktop. Release your finger to restore the open windows.

Keyboard and Mouse

Press the Windows logo key plus the comma key to preview the Desktop. To restore the previous view simply release the Windows logo key.

Tip 14-Windows Defender

Unlike previous versions, Windows 8 provides you with a basic level of security from the beginning. Windows Defender was previously only an Anti-spyware program but in Windows 8 it now includes Anti-virus protection. However, you can still choose to use security software if you want to.

Touch

Activate the Charms menu, tap Search and type "Windows Defender" and then tap to select it. Choose from Quick, Full and Custom scan types and then tap Scan now.

Keyboard

Press the Windows logo key plus the Q key and type "Windows Defender" and then click it. Choose from Quick, Full and Custom scan types and then click Scan now.

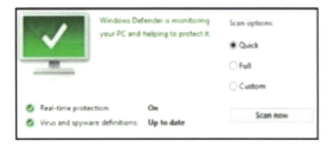

Tip 15-Shutdown

Microsoft doesn't want you to shut down your Windows 8 devices because of improved power management for older machines and a new feature known as "Connected Standby" which allows newer devices to stay connected to the net in sleep mode. However not everyone wants to leave their device on all the time and there are still ways to shut down.

Touch

Activate the Charms menu and select Settings, tap Power and select Shut down.

Keyboard

Press Ctrl plus Alt plus Del and click Power, then select Shut down.

Tip 16-Desktop Sync

When you sign in to Windows 8 with a Microsoft Account you can synchronize your Desktop settings for all of your Windows 8 PCs.

<u>Touch</u>

Activate the Charms menu and tap Search. Select Settings and type "Sync", then tap on Sync your settings.

<u>Keyboard and Mouse</u>

Press the Windows logo key plus W and type "Sync", then click on Sync your settings.

Tip 17-News App

The News app collects information from more than 175 of the world's leading news sites. You can customize your news topics with the My News feature. Open the News app, then swipe or right-click to activate the App bar. Tap or click on My News, select Add A Section and start typing a topic, tap or click Add or select a suggested topic from the list. To remove a topic, tap or click on the topic heading to show all its news results, then activate the App bar and select Remove section.

Tip 18-Weather App

The Weather App lets allows you to search and save your favorite places, so you quickly access them using the Places button at the top of the screen when you activate the App bars.

<u>Touch</u>

Open the Weather app and activate the Charms menu and tap Search. Type a location and select a result. Tap the Add button to save the location. You will now see a list of your saved locations when you activate the App bar and select Places.

Keyboard and Mouse

Open the Weather app and press the Windows logo key plus Q to activate the Search charm. Type a location and select a result. Click the Add button to save the location. You will now see a list of your saved locations when you activate the App bar and select Places.

Tip 19-Watchlist

With the Finance app you can check charts and statistics for stocks from around the world, get loan and currency rate data and check the latest economic news all in one place.

To add a stock to your Watchlist, open the Finance app, pan or scroll to the Watchlist, then tap or click the Add button and type in a stock symbol or company name, tap or click Add or select a suggested stock from the drop-down list. To remove an item from the Watchlist, just swipe-select or right-click on the stock and select Remove from the App bar.

Tip 20-Switching to a Microsoft Account

With Windows 8 you can use either a Local user account or a Microsoft account. With previous versions of Windows most consumers would have used a Local account, but now the preferred option is a Microsoft account. With a Microsoft account you can download apps from the Windows Store, sync your PC settings across multiple devices and access Microsoft's SkyDrive cloud service. If you have a Local account you can easily switch it to a Microsoft account.

Activate the Charms menu, select Settings and Change PC Settings. Then select Users and tap or click on the Switch to a Microsoft account button.

You can sign in with an existing Microsoft account or choose to sign up for a new email address.

Tip 21-Recover It

With Windows 8 you can create a system recovery drive that can be used to restore Windows if your system crashes.

To create a Recovery Drive, close all open files and apps, activate the Search Charm, select Settings and type "recovery". Tap or click on Create a recovery drive. Select Yes and Next, then connect a spare USB flash drive (existing date on the drive will be deleted). Tap or click on the Create button and when the recovery drive is ready, select Finish. Open File Explorer and select the drive in the navigation pane, then go to the Drive Tools tab and Eject the drive. Once this is done you should label and store the Recovery Drive in a safe place.

Tip 22-SkyDrive

The SkyDrive app gives you access to Microsoft's cloud storage, which lets you upload, sync and share files with your other devices. You will need a Microsoft account to use the SkyDrive app. To access SkyDrive directly from the Internet, go to http://skydrive.com. You can also use SkyDrive apps for Windows Phone, Android, Mac, iPhone and iPad.

Tip 23-Favorites

The Favorites button doesn't exist in the Modern interface. Bu you can still access your favorites from the New Tab button.

Touch

Swipe down from the top of the screen to show the App bar, then tap on the New Tab button. Your Favorites will be shown next to your frequently visited websites.

Keyboard and Mouse

Right click to activate the App bar and click on the New Tab button or use the shortcut Ctrl + T. Your Favorites will be shown next to your frequently visited websites.

Tip 24-Multi Monitor Taskbar

Windows 8 has improved the way the Taskbar works with multiple displays.

Touch

Long-press on an empty area of the Taskbar to activate the options menu, then tap Properties. Under the Multiple displays section you can change the appearance of the Taskbar.

Keyboard and Mouse

Right click on an empty space of the Taskbar to activate the options menu, then click Properties. Under the Multiple displays section you can change the appearance of the Taskbar.

Tip 25-Keyboard Shortcuts

This is a list of Windows 8 Keyboard Shortcuts. The categories are General, Acessibility, Charms, Desktop, and Semantic Zoom.

General

Windows logo key + D =Show Desktop

Windows logo key =Show Start Screen

Alt + Tab =Cycle between apps

Windows logo key + Tab =Show recent apps

Windows logo key + Z =Show app bars

Alt + F4 =Close apps

Windows logo key + , =Peek at the Desktop

Windows logo key + . =Snap Modern apps or the Desktop to the left of the screen

Windows logo key + L =Lock the screen

Windows logo key + O =Lock screen orientation

Ctrl + Alt + Del =Show the Windows Security Screen

Ctrl + Alt + Arrow Keys =Rotate the screen

Accessibility

Windows logo key + U =Ease of Access Center

Windows logo key + Enter =Narrator

Left Alt + Left Shit + PrtSc =High Contrast

Left Alt + Left Shit + NumLock =Mouse Keys

Hold NumLock for five seconds =Toggle Keys

Windows logo key + Plus Sign =Start Magnifier and zoom in

Windows logo key + Minus Sign =Start Magnifier and zoom out

Windows logo key + Escape =Exit Magnifier

Charms

Windows logo key + C = Show the Charms menu

Windows logo key + Q = Search for Apps

Windows logo key + W = Search for Settings

Windows logo key + F = Search for Files

Windows logo key + H = Show Share charm

Windows logo key + K = Show Device charm

Windows logo key + I = Show Settings charm

Desktop

Windows logo key + Left Arrow = Snap the active window to the left of the screen.

Windows logo key + Right Arrow = Snap the active window to the right of the screen.

Windows logo key + Up Arrow = Maximize window

Windows logo key + Down Arrow = Minimize window

Windows logo key + M = Minimize all windows

Semantic Zoom

Ctrl + Mouse Wheel = Semantic Zoom in Modern UI

Ctrl + Shift + Minus Sign = Zoom out

Ctrl + Shift + Plus Sign = Zoom in

Part 2

Introduction

Microsoft has its own digital distribution platform for Windows 8 and Windows RT. The Windows Store offers free and paid apps that can be downloaded onto computers and devices that use Microsoft's Windows 8 operating system. The Windows Store currently has more than 40,000 apps and that number is going to increase with developers submitting new apps.

The Windows Store is divided into many different categories including: Books & Reference, Business, Education, Entertainment, Finance, Food & Dining, Games, Government, Health & Fitness, Lifestyle, Music & Video, News & Weather, Photo, Productivity, Security, Shopping, Social, Sports, Tools and Travel.

App is short for application. An application is software that performs a specific task. The introduction of tablets and smartphones popularized the term app.

What is the difference between an app and a program? Apps usually are cheaper than programs. Also another difference is the way that apps are published, delivered and installed.

App 1-Youtube Downloader

With this you can download YouTube videos while you watch them. This app displays two buttons-one to save the video that is playing, and another to only save the audio.

App 2-Watchlist

This app helps you keep track of TV shows. You can browse and search for shows and you can get information about episodes, tweets about that show and other details.

App 3-Netflix

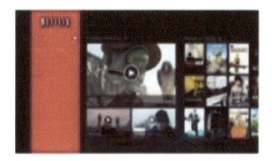

Netflix has released an app for Windows 8. For a low monthly fee you get unlimited streaming of their library of movies and TV shows.

App 4-News Bento

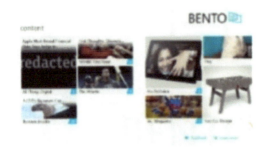

This app lets you view your favorite online news sources using a simple interface.

App 5-Podcasts

App 6-Tasks by Telerik

Tasks by Telerik is a colorful task manager with support for reminders and notifications, voice and photo notes, with Snap and Live Tiles options. This app will you to plan and stay organized.

App 7-Skype

The outstanding communications app is optimized for Windows 8 which is not very surprising considering that Skype is owned by Microsoft.

App 8-Popular Science

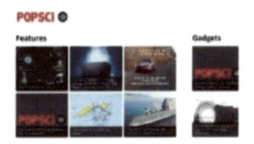

Popular Science covers everything science and technology and this app provides news and information on the latest innovations. You can browse for and check out articles and videos right from within the app.

App 9-Music Maker Jam

If you like to make music then this app is for you. You get access to four music Styles (jazz, dubstep, tech house and rock) with more available for a fee. After selecting a style you can manage the samples in the DJ control panel. Recorded tracks can be recorded as mp3 files.

App 10-Work Notes Pro

This is a notes and recording app that lets you text, image, audio and video clippings which can then be saved, searched, managed and shared. It also has Bing Maps, SkyDrive and Live ID integration.

App 11-Stumble Upon

If you are bored then this is an app for you. Clicking on the stumble button takes you to random websites based on your interests.

App 12-Piktr

If you like Instagram then this app is for you. For a small fee, Piktr brings the best Instagram experience on Windows 8, allowing you to browse through Instagram photos. Piktr is integrated with Microsoft's latest operating system with the ability to use Search Charms and Semantic Zoom.

App 13-Bing My Lockscreen

You can change the lock screen image in Windows 8 using the Settings menu but if you like surprises then this app is for you. Bing's search engines provide a new image every day and this app can collect that image every day and automatically set it as your lock screen background. You can also browse the last 8 images and do this by yourself manually.

App 14-Movieoholic

This app is all about movies. Clicking on a movie poster displays information about that movie as well as links to trailers on YouTube.

App 15-Tune in Radio

With this app you can listen to radio from around the world. You get access to over 60,000 radio stations and more than 2 million on demand programs.

App 16-Typo

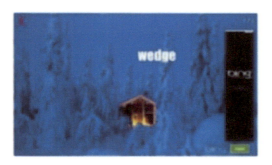

Maybe you could use some typing practice. This is a game with words falling down from the top and requiring you to type them before they reach the bottom. You can play this with a touchscreen or a keyboard.

App 17-Backgrounds Wallpapers HD

This app allows you to select images as wallpapers for your device's lock screen and account picture. With an option to save the photos, you can easily use the wallpapers as desktop backgrounds too.

App 18-Norton Satellite

Microsoft has increased security with Windows 8 but it is not a bad idea to add another layer of protection. Norton Satellite is a lightweight solution that scans your Facebook and Twitter feeds for malicious links. It also checks files stored on your Dropbox account for viruses and malware.

App 19-Storm

The Weather category has many different apps available however Storm is one that stands out due to its features and design. You can save different locations individually as separate tiles so you can get weather updates on your Start Screen.

App 20-FlipToast

Flip Toast allows you to integrate your social life-Facebook, Twitter, LinkedIn and Instagram-in one place. It has support for Live Tiles.

App 21-WorldWeb

This English dictionary and thesaurus app gives you the ability to look up word Definitions. World Web is free of advertisements and does not require an internet connection.

App 22-How Stuff Works

This app brings the content and YouTube videos from How Stuff Works.com right onto your screen. You can browse popular articles or watch video clips.

App 23-MultiMedia 8

This app can be used for a media player replacement for Windows 8. Multimedia 8 can play files locally or using network access, with support for subtitles, 3D video, and the ability to capture and convert media files.

App 24-USA Today

The USA Today app provides the latest news stories, sports scores, stock market information, photos, videos and weather.

App 25-CNN app for Windows

Do you like to keep up to date with all the latest news? Then this is an app for you. The CNN app has support for Live Tiles so news can be delivered to you on the Start Screen.

TERMS OF USE